WAYS INTO HISTORY

Brunel
The Great Engineer

Written by Sally Hewitt

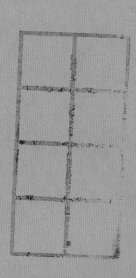

W

FRANKLIN WATTS
LONDON • SYDNEY

This edition 2012

First published in 2004 by
Franklin Watts
338 Euston Road
London NW1 3BH

Franklin Watts Australia
Level 17/207 Kent Street
Sydney NSW 2000

Series editor: Sally Luck
Art Director: Jonathan Hair
Design: Rachel Hamdi/Holly Mann
Picture Research: Diana Morris

A CIP catalogue record for this book is available
from the British Library.

Picture credits
Archivo Iconografico, S.A./ Corbis: 20; Ivan J Belcher/Worldwide Picture Library/Alamy Images: 15tl,
27; Bettmann/Corbis: 22t, 23c; Courtesy of Bristol City Museums & Art Galleries: 25;
British Museum/Bridgeman Art Library: 9cl; Chapman/Topham: 18r; Corporation of
London/HIP/Topham: 9cr; Mary Evans Picture Library: 13b, 18l, 21t; Fotomas/Topham: 14;
Tim Hawkins/Eye Ubiquitous/Corbis: 26t; HIP/Topham: 19; Rupert Horrox/Corbis: 6;
Hulton Archive: front cover br, 3, 9tl, 17t, 21c, 24; Hulton Collection/Corbis: 9tr, 17c;
Andrew Milligan/PA/Topham: 26b; National Railway Museum, York/Topham: front cover cl, 7, 8, 11;
Picturepoint/Topham: 10tl, 10c; Rolf Richardson/Alamy Images: 15c;
Science Museum, London/Topham: 12-13; Stapleton Collection/Corbis: 22b.

Every attempt has been made to clear copyright. Should there
be any inadvertent omission, please apply to
the publisher for rectification.

ISBN 978 1 4451 0960 2

Printed in China

Franklin Watts is a division of Hachette Children's Books,
an Hachette UK company.
www.hachette.co.uk

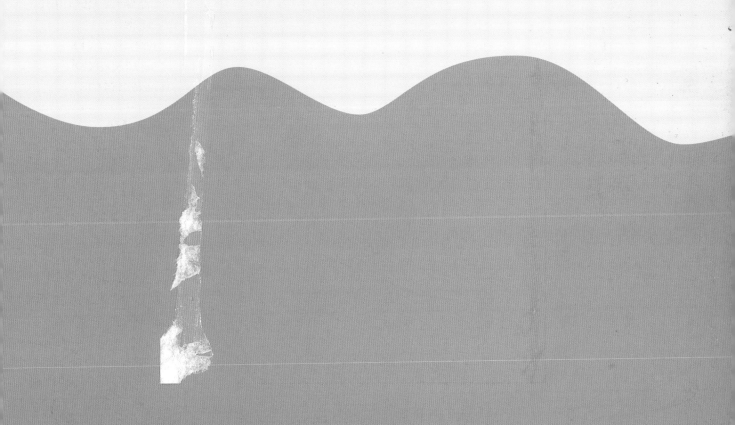

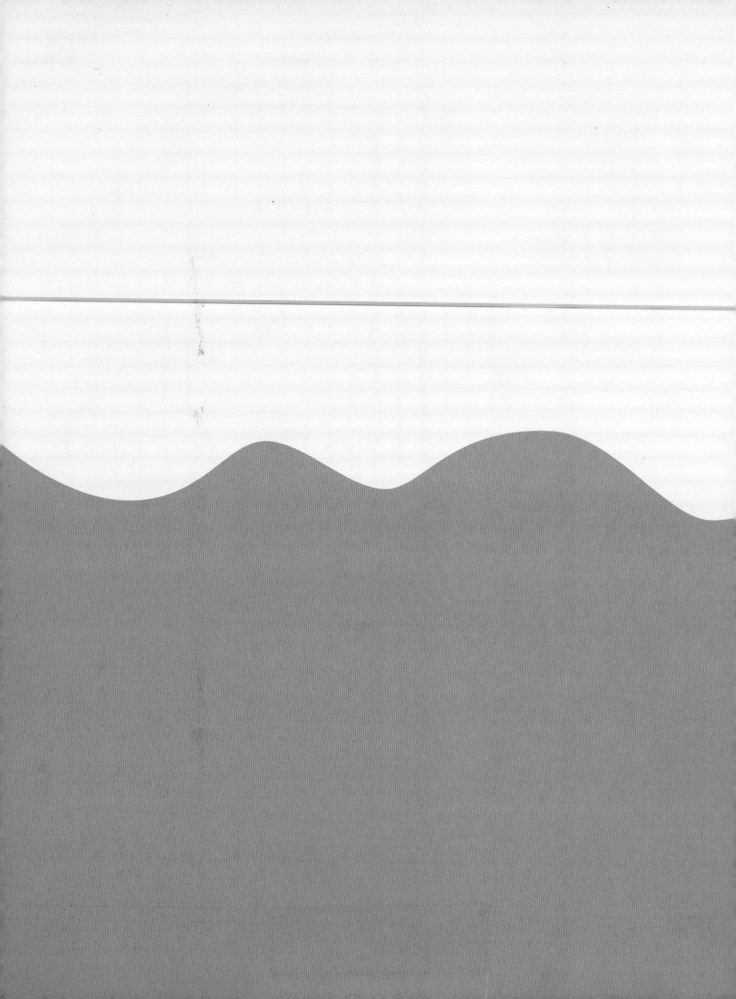

Contents

Whose statue is it?

There are statues of people all over the world. A statue of a person is put up so that they will always be remembered.

In Trafalgar Square, London, there is a statue of Admiral Lord Nelson. He won an important battle 200 years ago.

Why do you think Nelson's column is so tall?

Be a historian...

Look out for any statues where you live.

- Can you find out who the statue is of and why they were famous?
- How does a statue help us remember someone?

This is a statue of Isambard Kingdom Brunel. He was a famous engineer who lived over 100 years ago. An engineer plans and builds tunnels, bridges, trains, ships and buildings.

Born to be an engineer

Isambard Kingdom Brunel was born in 1806. His father was an engineer and he decided Isambard should be an engineer too!

◁ Isambard Kingdom Brunel

The young Brunel was good at mathematics and had exciting ideas.

What other skills would he need to be an engineer?

As an engineer, Brunel had to draw plans for his ideas. He had many other jobs to do, too.

Build!

Find skilled workers

Work out the cost

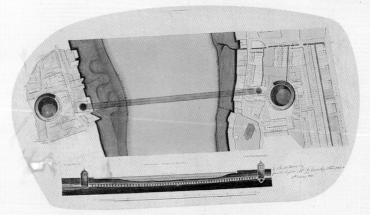
Draw the plans

Be a historian...

Look at the pictures above.

- Can you put these jobs in the correct order?
- What other jobs do you think Brunel had to do?

Victorian Britain

Brunel lived when Queen Victoria was on the throne. She reigned from 1837 to 1901.

Queen
Victoria

Victorian Britain was rich and powerful. There was money to spend on transport and new buildings.

△ A new Victorian Town Hall

Be a historian...

- Are there any Victorian buildings where you live? What do they look like?
- Why do you think Victorian Britain was an exciting time for a young engineer?

Victorian Britain was a time of inventions and change. New railways were built. Trains were becoming faster, cheaper and more comfortable.

△ North Western Railway, 1848

💬 Talk about...

... how people travelled before trains were invented. What forms of transport were invented after the train?

The first big project

Brunel joined his father's engineering business. His first big project was a tunnel under the river Thames.

△ The Thames Tunnel

◯ Be a historian ...

This tunnel was the first to be built under water.

- Why do you think no one had built an underwater tunnel before?
- Why was it such a difficult job?

One day, the tunnel flooded. Brunel helped his workers escape. He saved one man's life. Brunel's father invented a tunelling shield to make tunelling safer. It was made from iron.

How do you think the tunnelling shield protected the workers?

What do you think Brunel's next project was? Turn the page to find out...

△ The tunelling shield

The Clifton Suspension Bridge

Brunel broke his leg working in the Thames Tunnel. While recovering in hospital, he won a competition to design a bridge over the river Avon at Bristol.

Brunel's winning design

Brunel designed a suspension bridge – the first of its kind. It was supported by towers at each end and hung from cables in the middle.

Brunel called the bridge "my first child, my darling". What do you think he meant?

The towers on either side of the river Avon were built - but then the money ran out.

The Clifton Suspension Bridge today

The bridge was not finished until 1864, after Brunel died. Traffic has been crossing it ever since.

Be a historian...

- What differences can you spot between Brunel's design and the bridge now?
- Why do you think the bridge is so famous?

The Great Western Railway

Railways were being built all over Victorian Britain. In 1833, Brunel was given the job of building the Great Western Railway, between London and Bristol.

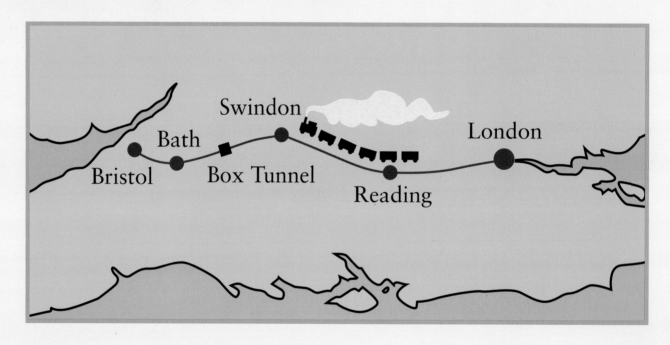

⚲ Be a historian...

Brunel rode on horseback from London to Bristol, making his plans for the railway line.

• Why do you think he did this?

• What tools do you think he took with him?

Brunel designed Box Tunnel along the route. It was the longest tunnel in the country. Men tunnelled from each end and met in the middle.

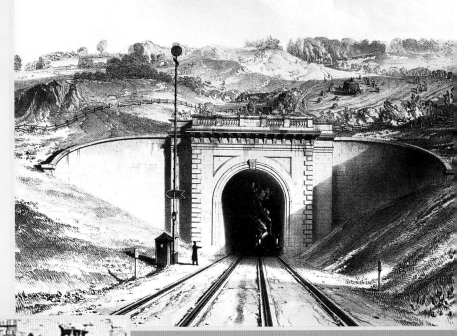

Dynamite was used to blast the tunnel through the hillside. More than a hundred workers died.

Talk about...

. . . how it would feel to work in Box Tunnel.

Use these words to help you:

dark   stuffy   frightened   crowded

Queen Victoria takes the train

Brunel wanted travelling by train to be fast, comfortable and safe. His dream was to make the ride so smooth that passengers could drink coffee without it spilling.

A Victorian train

A modern train

Be a historian...

- What materials were used inside Brunel's train carriages?
- What materials are used inside modern carriages?
- What other differences can you see?

In 1842, Queen Victoria chose to travel on the Great Western Railway. It was her first train ride. Brunel boasted that his railway was "the finest work in England".

Why was this such a great day for Brunel? Which famous person today might he want to ride on his train?

💬 Talk about...
. . . what it would be like to travel on a steam train.
What would you see, hear and smell?
Use these words to help you:
smoke   steam   coal   burning   whistle   engine

Across the sea

Brunel decided to build a ship to cross the Atlantic Ocean faster than ever before...

Before Brunel's steamships, only sailing boats made long journeys. Steamships used coal as fuel. They could not carry enough coal to travel very far.

◁ A sailing ship

Why couldn't ships carry a lot of fuel?

In 1836, Brunel built a big, wooden steamship called the *Great Western*. It could stand up to storms and carry enough fuel to cross the Atlantic.

In 1858, he built the *Great Eastern*. It was made of metal and was the biggest ship in the world!

◁ The *Great Eastern*

🔍 Be a historian...

Look at the three ships on this page.

- How are they different?
- How are they similar?

The Crimea

In 1854, Great Britain went to war with Russia in the Crimea. Wounded British soldiers were dying in dirty, crowded hospitals.

Talk about...

. . . what it would be like in these hospitals. Use these words to help you:

dirty   smelly   frightening   crowded

A nurse called Florence Nightingale went to help. She worked hard to make the hospitals clean and safe. How do you think she did this?

Brunel was asked to help. He designed the first prefabricated hospital. All the parts were made in Britain, shipped to the Crimea and put together on the spot.

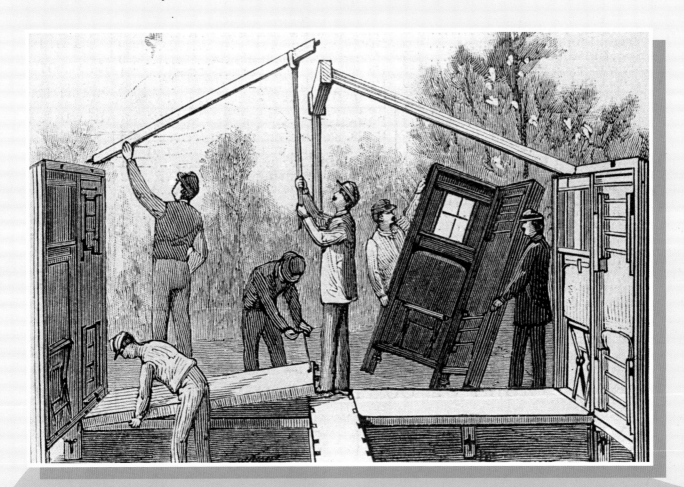

Be a historian...

Brunel's plans included:

lavatories   baths   wash basins   drains

- Very few wounded soldiers died in Brunel's hospital. How do you think his design helped to save soldiers' lives?

Hard work and adventure

Brunel worked hard all his life. He didn't only sit in an office making plans and giving orders. He went to where the work was being done and he joined in!

Be a historian ...

Look carefully at Brunel's trousers and boots.

- What tells you that he got involved in the job?
- How does Brunel look different from the portrait on page 8?

Brunel had many dangerous adventures. When the Clifton Suspension Bridge was being built, he rode across the River Avon in a basket.

It got stuck half way across. Brunel had to climb out and fix it himself!

💬 Talk about...

. . . what kind of person you think Brunel was.
Use these words to help you:

brave   adventurous   hard working

clever   talented   inventive

Why do we remember Brunel?

Brunel broke many records. He built the biggest ship in the world and the longest underground tunnel.

His ideas helped future engineers invent things like the Channel Tunnel and the Queen Mary 2.

△ The Channel Tunnel

▽ The Queen Mary 2

Many of Brunel's designs are still being used today, more than 150 years later.

Trains still travel over the Royal Albert Bridge at Tamar in Cornwall. Brunel built this in 1859.

The Royal Albert Bridge

Be a historian...

Look back though the book. Can you find...

- ... some of Brunel's work that helped to make the modern designs on page 26 possible?
- ... some of Brunel's designs that are still used today?

Find out about other works of Brunel that you can go to see.

Timeline

1806
Brunel is born in Portsmouth, 9th April.

1822
Brunel starts to work for his father.

Start

1827
The Thames Tunnel is flooded and Brunel is injured.

1830
Brunel designs the Clifton Suspension Bridge.

1833
Brunel becomes chief engineer on the Great Western Railway.

1838
The *Great Western* crosses the Atlantic.

1841
The Great Western Railway is opened.

1842
Queen Victoria takes her first train ride.

1855
Brunel's prefabricated hospital is built in the Crimea.

1859
Brunel dies, 15th September.

1858
The *Great Eastern* is built.

End

Glossary

Business
The work people do
to earn money.

Engineer
Someone who plans
and builds tunnels,
machines, bridges,
ships and buildings.

Invention
A new idea for a design
that no one has
thought of before.

Materials
What things are made
of, such as iron, cloth
and wood.

Prefabricated
All the parts of a
prefabricated building
are made in a factory.
They are put together
on the building site.

Reign
To rule as a king
or a queen.

Statue
A sculpture put up in
memory of someone
important.

Transport
Cars, aeroplanes, trains
and ships are all kinds
of transport. Transport
carries people from
place to place.

Index